CYBERSECURITY FROM A TO Z

EVERYTHING YOU NEED TO KNOW TO PROTECT YOURSELF AND YOUR ORGANIZATION

JOHN BEJTRAVITCH

Copyright © 2023 by John BEJTRAVITCH. All Right Reserved.

No part of this publication may be reproduced, distributed, or transmitted in any form or by any means or by any information storage and retrieval system without the prior written permission of the publisher, except in the case of very brief quotations embodied in critical reviews and certain other noncommercial uses permitted by copyright law.

Table of Contents

Introduction

Chapter 1: Understanding Cybersecurity

Chapter 2: Types of Cyber Threats

Chapter 3: Protecting Personal Data

Chapter 4: Protecting Business Data

Chapter 5: Preventing Cyberattacks

Chapter 6: Detecting Cyberattacks

Chapter 7: Responding to Cyberattacks

Chapter 8: Cybersecurity Trends and Developments

Conclusion

Introduction

In today's world, technology plays an integral role in our daily lives. From online banking and shopping to social media and online communication, the internet has become an integral part of how we live and work. However, with the increasing use of technology comes an increased risk of cybercrime. Cybersecurity is a term used to describe the protection of data, systems, and networks from unauthorized access, theft, and damage. It is the practice of securing computers, servers, mobile devices, electronic systems, networks, and data from cyber threats and attacks.

The importance of cybersecurity cannot be overstated. With more and more sensitive information being stored and transmitted online, the risks of data breaches, identity theft, and financial loss are greater than ever. Whether it's a personal or a business context, the consequences of a cyberattack can be devastating. Data theft can result in sensitive information being leaked, financial losses can be incurred due to unauthorized transactions, and the damage to an organization's reputation can be irreparable.

Cybersecurity is not just a concern for businesses, but for individuals as well. As we continue to live more of our lives online, it's essential that we take the necessary precautions to protect ourselves and our information. From setting strong passwords and being cautious when sharing personal information online to using antivirus software and avoiding suspicious emails, there are many steps that individuals can take to protect themselves from cyber threats.

Despite the growing awareness of the importance of cybersecurity, many people are still not taking the necessary precautions to protect themselves and their information. This is largely due to a lack of understanding about what cybersecurity entails and the steps that can be taken to protect against cyber threats. That's why this book has been created - to provide a comprehensive guide to cybersecurity from A to Z.

The book will cover all aspects of cybersecurity, from the basics of what it entails to the types of cyber threats and attacks, best practices for protecting personal and business data, and ways to prevent, detect, and respond to cyberattacks. It will also touch on the latest trends and developments in cybersecurity and how these will impact individuals and businesses in the future.

It is a comprehensive guide to understanding and protecting against the various threats facing digital data today. In this book, we aim to provide you with a comprehensive overview of cybersecurity, from its definition and the different types of data that can be vulnerable to cyberattacks, to the best practices for protecting personal and business data, and responding to cyberattacks.

The book is designed to be accessible and informative, providing readers with a thorough understanding of cybersecurity and the steps they can take to protect themselves and their information.

The book is divided into several chapters, each focusing on a different aspect of cybersecurity:

The first chapter, "Understanding Cybersecurity," defines the term and explains what it entails. We will discuss the different types of data that can be vulnerable to cyberattacks and the consequences of a successful attack, including data theft, financial loss, and damage to reputation.

Chapter 2, "Types of Cyber Threats," delves into the various types of cyber threats, including viruses, worms, trojans, ransomware, and phishing. We will explain how each threat works and what damage it can cause, as well as the methods used by cybercriminals to spread these threats.

In "Protecting Personal Data" (Chapter 3), we will cover the best practices for protecting personal data online, including using strong passwords, enabling two-factor authentication, and using antivirus software. We will also discuss the importance of being cautious when sharing personal information online, and the dangers of using public Wi-Fi. In addition, we will provide guidance on how to safeguard sensitive data stored on personal devices, such as laptops and smartphones.

Chapter 4, "Protecting Business Data," will explain the importance of protecting business data and the consequences of a data breach. We will discuss the best practices for securing business networks, including implementing firewalls, using encryption, and conducting regular security audits. We will also emphasize the role of employees in protecting business data and the importance of providing cybersecurity training.

In "Preventing Cyberattacks" (Chapter 5), we will discuss the steps that can be taken to prevent cyberattacks, including using strong passwords, keeping software up-to-date, and avoiding suspicious emails and websites. We will also explain the importance of conducting regular security audits and performing penetration testing, as well as the role of cybersecurity professionals in preventing cyberattacks and the importance of hiring a professional to assess security risks.

"Detecting Cyberattacks" (Chapter 6) will cover the signs that a cyberattack is underway, including unusual activity on a network, slow performance, and unusual emails. We will discuss the tools used by cybersecurity professionals to detect cyberattacks, including intrusion detection systems and network monitoring software, and emphasize the importance of having a plan in place for responding to a cyberattack, as well as the role of cybersecurity professionals in detecting and responding to threats.

Chapter 7, "Responding to Cyberattacks," will discuss the steps that should be taken to respond to a cyberattack, including isolating affected systems, conducting a forensic investigation, and restoring normal operations. We will also explain the importance of reporting cyberattacks to law enforcement and the role of cybersecurity professionals in responding to and resolving security incidents. Finally, we will provide guidance on the steps that can be taken to prevent similar attacks in the future, including implementing security measures and conducting regular security audits.

The final chapter, "Cybersecurity Trends and Developments," will cover the latest trends and developments in cybersecurity, including cloud security, artificial intelligence, and the Internet of Things (IoT). We will discuss the challenges and opportunities that these trends present for businesses and individuals, as well as the importance of staying up-to-date on cybersecurity trends and developments, and the role of cybersecurity professionals in staying ahead of the curve.

By the end of this book, you will have a comprehensive understanding of cybersecurity and the steps you can take to protect yourself and your information from cyber threats. Whether you're an individual looking to protect your personal data or a business owner looking to secure your network, this book will provide the knowledge and guidance you need to stay safe in today's digital world.

Chapter 1. Understanding Cybersecurity

Part 1: Defining Cybersecurity

Cybersecurity is a broad field that encompasses all the measures taken to protect digital information and assets from unauthorized access, use, disclosure, disruption, modification, or destruction. In a world that is becoming increasingly digital, cybersecurity is more important than ever. With the rise of the Internet, the number of connected devices, and the increasing use of cloud computing, people and organizations are facing new and more sophisticated cyber threats.

Cybersecurity is not just about protecting against hacking or data breaches. It encompasses a wide range of activities and technologies designed to protect against a variety of threats, including viruses, malware, phishing scams, and cyberattacks. These threats can take many forms, from simple viruses that infect a single computer to complex attacks that target entire organizations. In order to effectively protect against these threats, it's important to understand what cybersecurity is and what it entails.

Cybersecurity encompasses a number of different areas, including network security, application security, data security, and information security. Each of these areas involves different strategies and technologies designed to protect against specific types of threats. For example, network security focuses on protecting the networks that connect computers and devices, while application security focuses on protecting the software and applications that run on those devices. Data security focuses on protecting the data stored on those devices, while information security focuses on protecting the information contained within that data.

Cybersecurity also involves a number of different actors, including individuals, organizations, and governments. Each of these actors plays a role in protecting against cyber threats and has a different set of responsibilities and obligations. For example, individuals are responsible for protecting their own personal data and information, while organizations are responsible for protecting their employees and customers. Governments have a responsibility to protect the citizens and critical infrastructure of their country.

Cybersecurity is a constantly evolving field, and new threats and technologies are emerging all the time. In order to effectively protect against these threats, it's important to stay up-to-date on the latest developments in the field and to understand the different types of data that can be vulnerable to cyberattacks. In the next section of this chapter, we will explore the different types of data that can be vulnerable to cyberattacks, and why it is so important to protect them.

Part 2: Types of Data Vulnerable to Cyberattacks

As technology continues to advance, the types of data that are vulnerable to cyberattacks are becoming increasingly diverse. The following are some of the most common types of data that are at risk of being compromised by cybercriminals:

Personal Information: This includes sensitive information such as social security numbers, credit card numbers, bank account information, and other personally identifiable information (PII). This type of data is highly sought after by cybercriminals who use it to steal identities, commit fraud, and other types of financial crimes.

Financial Information: Financial data is another type of data that is vulnerable to cyberattacks. This includes information related to bank accounts, credit card numbers, and other financial transactions. Cybercriminals can use this information to steal money or commit fraud.

Health Information: Health information is a type of data that is becoming increasingly vulnerable to cyberattacks. This includes personal health information such as medical records, diagnoses, and treatments. Cybercriminals can use this information for a variety of purposes, including insurance fraud, identity theft, and other financial crimes.

Intellectual Property: Intellectual property is another type of data that is vulnerable to cyberattacks. This includes trade secrets, patents, trademarks, and other proprietary information. Cybercriminals can use this information to steal ideas, create fake products, or sell stolen intellectual property on the black market.

Sensitive Business Information: Sensitive business information is another type of data that is vulnerable to cyberattacks. This includes business plans, customer information, financial information, and other confidential data. Cybercriminals can use this information to steal business secrets, compromise customer data, and commit other types of financial crimes.

Government Information: Government information is also vulnerable to cyberattacks. This includes sensitive information such as classified documents, intelligence reports, and other government secrets. Cybercriminals can use this information to steal sensitive information, disrupt government operations, or commit other types of cybercrimes.

Social Media Information: Social media information is another type of data that is vulnerable to cyberattacks. This includes personal information such as social media profiles, private messages, and other sensitive information. Cybercriminals can use this information to steal identities, commit fraud, or use it for other types of cybercrimes.

Cyber-physical Systems: Cyber-physical systems are becoming increasingly vulnerable to cyberattacks as well. This includes critical infrastructure such as power grids, water systems, and transportation systems. Cybercriminals can use these systems to disrupt critical infrastructure, cause physical damage, or even cause loss of life.

Digital Certificates: Digital certificates are used to secure online transactions and are becoming increasingly vulnerable to cyberattacks. Cybercriminals can use these certificates to impersonate legitimate organizations and steal sensitive information or commit other types of cybercrimes.

Cloud Data: Cloud data is another type of data that is becoming increasingly vulnerable to cyberattacks. This includes data stored on cloud-based systems such as Amazon Web Services, Microsoft Azure, and Google Cloud. Cybercriminals can use this data to steal sensitive information, disrupt cloud-based systems, or commit other types of cybercrimes.

These are just a few examples of the types of data that are vulnerable to cyberattacks. As technology continues to advance, the types of data that are vulnerable to cyberattacks will only continue to grow. It is important for organizations and individuals to understand the risks and take steps to protect their data.

Part 3: Consequences of a Cyberattack

A cyberattack can have far-reaching consequences for both individuals and organizations. The impact of a cyberattack can range from simple inconvenience to serious harm, such as financial loss and damage to reputation. Understanding the consequences of a cyberattack is essential for taking the necessary precautions to protect against cyber threats.

One of the most common consequences of a cyberattack is data theft. In many cases, cybercriminals target sensitive information, such as personal information, financial information, and confidential business data. The theft of sensitive information can have serious consequences, including identity theft and financial fraud. For businesses, the theft of confidential information can also damage their reputation and cause long-term financial losses.

Another common consequence of a cyberattack is financial loss. Cyberattacks can cause direct financial losses through theft or fraud, as well as indirect financial losses due to lost productivity, damage to equipment, and loss of business. For example, a ransomware attack can encrypt important data and demand payment to restore access. In some cases, organizations may be forced to pay the ransom to regain access to their data, resulting in significant financial losses.

A cyberattack can also damage an organization's reputation. The public is becoming increasingly aware of the threat of cyberattacks, and any data breaches or security incidents can have a significant impact on an organization's reputation. For example, customers may choose to do business with a competitor if they perceive the organization to be less secure.

A cyberattack can also damage an organization's reputation in the eyes of investors, suppliers, and other stakeholders.

Finally, a cyberattack can cause operational disruption. A cyberattack can cause systems to crash, resulting in lost productivity and the inability to access critical data. This can cause significant inconvenience and delay for organizations, as well as for individuals. For example, a hospital may be unable to access patient records, leading to delays in treatment and potentially putting lives at risk.

In conclusion, the consequences of a cyberattack can be severe and far-reaching, impacting both individuals and organizations. Protecting against cyber threats requires an understanding of the types of data that are vulnerable to cyberattacks, as well as the consequences of a breach. By taking the necessary precautions and being aware of the potential consequences of a cyberattack, individuals and organizations can minimize the risks and protect against cyber threats.

Chapter 2. Types of Cyber Threats

Part 1: Different Types of Cyber Threats

Cyber threats come in many forms and are constantly evolving. It is essential for individuals and organizations to understand the various types of threats and the harm they can cause. In this section, we will discuss five of the most common types of cyber threats: viruses, worms, trojans, ransomware, and phishing.

Viruses: A computer virus is a malicious software program that infects a computer system and replicates itself by inserting a copy of itself into other programs or files. Viruses can cause a range of problems, from slowing down your computer to deleting or corrupting files. They are often spread through email attachments, infected software downloads, and other means of file transfer.

Worms: A worm is a type of malware that spreads from computer to computer without the need for human interaction. Unlike viruses, worms can spread on their own without being attached to a file. They often exploit vulnerabilities in computer systems and networks to spread quickly, causing significant damage in a short amount of time.

Trojans: Trojans are malicious software programs that are disguised as legitimate software. They are designed to give hackers remote access to a computer system, allowing them to steal sensitive information or cause damage. Trojans can be spread through email attachments, infected software downloads, and other means of file transfer.

Ransomware: Ransomware is a type of malware that encrypts a victim's files and demands a ransom payment in exchange for the decryption key. Ransomware attacks can be particularly devastating for organizations, as they can result in the loss of critical data and significant downtime.

Phishing: Phishing is a type of social engineering attack that aims to trick victims into providing sensitive information or downloading malicious software. Phishing attacks often take the form of fake emails or websites that appear to be from trusted organizations, and they may contain links that lead to malicious websites or downloads.

These five types of cyber threats are just a few examples of the many types of threats that exist. It is essential for individuals and organizations to understand the different types of cyber threats and to be aware of the methods that cybercriminals use to spread them. By being proactive and taking appropriate measures to protect their systems and networks, individuals and organizations can reduce their risk of becoming a victim of a cyber attack.

PART 2: UNDERSTANDING THE TYPES OF CYBER THREATS AND THEIR EFFECTS

In Part 1, we briefly introduced the five main types of cyber threats: viruses, worms, trojans, ransomware, and phishing. But it's important to dive deeper into each threat to understand how they work and what damage they can cause.

Viruses: A virus is a type of malicious software (malware) that infects a computer or device and spreads to other devices. The main aim of a virus is to cause harm to the infected device or network, and the extent of harm can vary greatly. It is important to understand the nature of viruses in order to prevent them from causing damage to your device or network.

Viruses are typically spread through email attachments, software downloads, or other means. For example, a user might receive an email that appears to come from a reputable source and includes an attachment. When the user opens the attachment, the virus is installed on their device and can then spread to other devices on the network. This type of virus can be particularly dangerous because it can infect multiple devices at once, making it difficult to stop the spread of the virus.

In addition to spreading to other devices, viruses can also cause harm to the infected device. For example, a virus can slow down the performance of the device or steal sensitive information. In some cases, viruses can also infect and delete important files, making it difficult or impossible to recover lost data. For instance, imagine you had a critical report due the next day and your computer gets infected with a virus that deletes all your files, this can lead to missed deadlines and negative consequences for your professional or personal life. To prevent the spread of viruses, it is crucial to keep all software and security systems up-to-date and to avoid opening suspicious emails or downloading software from unknown sources.

Worms: A type of malware that is different from viruses, worms are self-replicating programs that spread themselves without any human intervention. Unlike viruses, they don't need to attach themselves to a file, rather they exploit security vulnerabilities in operating systems and software to infect a computer and spread to other devices in a network.

One of the most common examples of a worm is the infamous "Code Red" worm, which attacked web servers in 2001. The worm was able to spread rapidly, infecting thousands of servers within a matter of hours. It consumed significant amounts of network bandwidth, slowing down system performance and causing widespread downtime for affected networks.

The impact of worms can be devastating for businesses and organizations, as it can cause significant damage to computer systems and networks. Worms can allow unauthorized access to sensitive information and cause widespread system crashes, leading to downtime, lost productivity, and financial losses. This is why it is important for businesses to take measures to protect their systems against worm attacks, such as regularly updating software and operating systems, and implementing robust firewalls and intrusion detection systems.

Trojans: they are often disguised as legitimate software programs, making them hard to detect. Unlike other forms of malware, Trojans do not spread on their own and must be manually installed by the user, usually through a deceptive method such as a fake software update or a seemingly harmless attachment in an email.

Once installed on a computer, Trojans are designed to steal sensitive information, such as passwords, credit card numbers, and other personal data. For example, a Trojan may appear to be a simple game, but it could secretly be collecting the user's login information for financial websites. In addition to stealing information, Trojans can also be used to install additional malware, such as spyware, on the infected computer. This spyware can monitor the user's activity and gather sensitive information without the user's knowledge.

The danger of Trojans lies in their ability to go undetected for extended periods of time. This allows attackers to gather sensitive information over a long period, increasing the amount of damage they can cause. Furthermore, Trojans can also be used to install more dangerous malware, such as ransomware, which can lock a user's files and demand a ransom payment to unlock them. In short, Trojans are a serious threat to the security of personal and business data, and it is important to be aware of them and take steps to protect against them.

Ransomware:

Ransomware is a malicious software that has become a growing concern for both individuals and organizations alike. The primary objective of ransomware is to encrypt the user's data, making it inaccessible without paying a ransom fee. This type of malware can spread through a variety of means, including email attachments, malicious links, and infected software downloads. Once the computer or network is infected, the attackers will demand payment in exchange for the decryption key that would allow the user to access their data.

Ransomware attacks can cause significant damage to an organization's operations, as the encryption of critical data can result in downtime and the loss of important information. In some cases, the malware can infect an entire network, making it nearly impossible to access important data and systems. This can lead to a complete disruption of business operations, causing significant financial losses and damage to a company's reputation. In addition to the immediate consequences, the aftermath of a ransomware attack can be just as damaging, as businesses may struggle to regain the trust of their customers and partners.

While the temptation to pay the ransom may be strong, it is important to understand that there is no guarantee that the attackers will provide the decryption key, even if the ransom is paid. In some cases, the attackers may demand additional payments or continue to threaten the user with further attacks. Additionally, paying the ransom can also encourage the attackers to continue their malicious activities, as they are motivated by financial gain. Therefore, it is important to have a comprehensive cybersecurity plan in place to prevent the occurrence of a ransomware attack, as well as having backup measures in place to recover critical data in the event of an attack.

Phishing is a highly sophisticated form of cyberattack that tricks individuals into giving away confidential information. The primary goal of a phishing attack is to steal sensitive information, such as login credentials, credit card numbers, and other personal data. In order to achieve this, attackers use emails, text messages, or phone calls that are designed to look as if they are from a trusted source, such as a bank, a well-known company, or a government agency.

Phishing scams can be very difficult to detect, even for experienced users. Attackers often use social engineering tactics, such as creating a sense of urgency, to convince individuals to act quickly and provide sensitive information. For example, an attacker might send an email that appears to come from a bank and warns the recipient that their account has been compromised. The email then provides a link to a fake login page, where the user is prompted to enter their login credentials.

The consequences of a successful phishing attack can be severe. In addition to the theft of sensitive information, phishing attacks can also result in the compromise of user accounts, the spread of malware to other devices, and significant financial losses. Moreover, the reputation of the targeted organization may also be tarnished, as individuals and businesses may lose trust in the security of their sensitive information. It is important for individuals and organizations to be vigilant against phishing scams and to take the necessary steps to protect themselves against this type of cyberattack. This can include implementing strong password policies, using two-factor authentication, and being cautious of unexpected emails or messages that request sensitive information.

PART 3: UNCOVERING THE TACTICS OF CYBERCRIMINALS: AN EXPLORATION OF THREAT PROPAGATION METHODS.

Cybercriminals are constantly seeking new ways to spread their malicious software and steal sensitive information. Understanding the methods used by these cybercriminals is essential for organizations and individuals to protect themselves from these types of attacks. In this section, we will take an in-depth look at the various methods used by cybercriminals to spread malware and compromise user accounts.

One of the most common methods used by cybercriminals to spread threats is through **email attachments.** Cybercriminals often send emails with a seemingly harmless attachment, such as an invoice, a PDF document, or a photo. When the recipient opens the attachment, the malware is installed on their computer, compromising their data and potentially spreading to other devices on the same network. To avoid falling victim to this type of attack, it is important to exercise caution when opening email attachments, especially from unknown or suspicious sources.

Another common method used by cybercriminals to spread threats is through **malicious links.** Cybercriminals may send emails, text messages, or instant messages with a link to a fake website that looks like a legitimate one, such as a bank or an online retailer. When the user enters their login information on the fake website, their sensitive information is captured by the cybercriminals, who can then use it for fraudulent purposes. It is important to be wary of links from unknown or suspicious sources and to double-check the URL before entering any sensitive information.

Social engineering is another popular method used by cybercriminals to spread threats. This technique involves tricking the victim into performing an action that allows the cybercriminal to compromise their device, such as downloading malware or revealing sensitive information. For example, a cybercriminal might call a victim posing as a technical support representative and ask them to download a software update that is actually malware. Another example is a phishing email that claims to be from a trusted source and asks the recipient to update their account information, when in reality it is a trap to steal their sensitive information.

Drive-by downloads are another method used by cybercriminals to spread threats. This technique involves exploiting vulnerabilities in web browsers or other software to automatically download and install malware onto the victim's computer without their knowledge or consent. For example, if a user visits a compromised website, the malware can be automatically downloaded and installed on their computer, compromising their data and potentially spreading to other devices on the same network. To avoid falling victim to this type of attack, it is important to keep all software up-to-date and to only visit trusted websites.

Lastly, cybercriminals may also spread threats through **infected software downloads**. This can occur when the victim downloads software from a malicious website or a peer-to-peer network that has been infected with malware. The malware can then infect the victim's computer, compromising their data and potentially spreading to other devices on the same network. To avoid falling victim to this type of attack, it is important to only download software from trusted sources and to regularly scan all downloads for malware.

To sum up, there are many methods used by cybercriminals to spread their malicious software and steal sensitive information. It is important to be aware of these methods and to take steps to protect oneself from these types of attacks. By exercising caution when opening email attachments, avoiding malicious links, being wary of social engineering attempts, keeping software up-to-date, and only downloading software from trusted sources, individuals and organizations can reduce their risk of falling victim to a cyber attack.

Chapter 3. Protecting Personal Data

Part 1: How to Keep Your Online Personal Data Safe and Secure

In the current technological era, personal information has become a sought-after asset. Every time you log into a website, make an online purchase, or use your smartphone, you are sharing your personal information with the world. Unfortunately, cybercriminals are always on the lookout for ways to steal your data and use it for their own gain. That's why it's important to take steps to protect your personal data online.

One of the best ways to protect your personal data is to use **strong passwords**. A strong password should be at least 12 characters long and include a mix of letters, numbers, and symbols. It's also important to avoid using easily guessable information, such as your name or birthdate, in your password.

Another way to protect your personal data online is to enable **two-factor authentication** (2FA). 2FA adds an extra layer of security to your accounts by requiring you to enter a code sent to your phone in addition to your password. This makes it much more difficult for cybercriminals to access your accounts, even if they know your password.

Using **antivirus software** is also an important step in protecting your personal data online. Antivirus software can detect and remove malware, such as viruses, worms, and trojans, which can steal your personal information. Make sure to keep your antivirus software up-to-date, as new threats are constantly being discovered.

To further illustrate the importance of these best practices, let's look at some real-world examples of how cybercriminals use passwords and other personal information to steal sensitive data. In 2016, a massive data breach at Yahoo affected all 3 billion of the company's user accounts. The hackers stole user names, email addresses, phone numbers, birthdates, and security questions and answers. This information was then used to access the accounts of other online services, such as banks and retailers.

Similarly, in 2017, the Equifax data breach impacted 143 million US consumers. The hackers were able to steal names, addresses, Social Security numbers, birthdates, and drivers license numbers, which they then sold on the dark web. The breach was a result of Equifax's failure to patch a vulnerability in its website, which allowed the hackers to access the sensitive data.

These examples highlight the importance of using strong passwords and other best practices to protect your personal data online. By taking these steps, you can help prevent your information from falling into the hands of cybercriminals and being used for malicious purposes.

Part 2: The Dangers of Sharing Personal Information Online and Public Wi-Fi

When it comes to protecting personal data, it's not only about securing our devices, but also about being mindful of what information we share online and how we access the internet. In this part, we will discuss the importance of being cautious when sharing personal information online and the dangers of using public Wi-Fi.

Personal information has become a valuable commodity in the digital age, and cybercriminals are always on the lookout for ways to get their hands on it. As such, it's important to be mindful of what information we share online and with whom.

For example, social media platforms like Facbook and Twitter can be a treasure trove of personal information for cybercriminals if we're not careful. They can use this information to steal our identities, commit fraud, or even blackmail us. Here are some tips for keeping our personal information safe on social media:

Be mindful of what information you post online, and avoid sharing sensitive information like your full name, address, phone number, or financial information. Be careful about who you accept friend requests from and who you share information with.

Adjust your privacy settings to limit the amount of information that is visible to others. Be careful about what third-party apps you grant access to your social media accounts.

Public Wi-Fi networks are often seen as a convenient way to access the internet on the go, but they can also be a security nightmare. Public Wi-Fi networks are often unsecured, meaning that anyone with the right tools can easily intercept your data and steal sensitive information like passwords and credit card numbers.

To stay safe when using public Wi-Fi, here are some tips:

- Avoid using public Wi-Fi for sensitive activities like online banking or shopping.
- If you must use public Wi-Fi, make sure to connect to a secure network that requires a password.
- Use a virtual private network (VPN) to encrypt your internet connection and protect your data.
- Be wary of free Wi-Fi hotspots, as they may be fake networks set up by cybercriminals to steal your information.

Ultimately, protecting personal information online requires more than just securing our devices. It also means being mindful of what we share online and how we access the internet. By being cautious when sharing personal information and avoiding the dangers of public Wi-Fi, we can take a major step towards protecting our privacy and security in the digital age.

Part 3: Protecting Sensitive Data on Personal Devices: Best Practices and Strategies

In order to ensure the protection of confidential information stored on personal devices like laptops and smartphones, it is crucial to follow a set of guidelines that have proven to be effective. Firstly, it's important to **lock your device with a secure password or PIN code** to prevent unauthorized access. This is the most basic yet essential step to protect your sensitive data stored on these devices.

Another important step is to **encrypt the data** stored on these devices. Encryption is the process of converting data into a code to protect its confidentiality. This way, even if someone gains access to your device, they will not be able to read your sensitive data. There are various encryption tools available, such as BitLocker for Windows and FileVault for MacOS, that make it easy to encrypt your data.

It's also important to regularly **backup your data**, so that you don't lose it in case of theft, loss, or device malfunction. This can be done through cloud storage services like Google Drive or Dropbox, or through external hard drives. By backing up your data regularly, you can ensure that your sensitive information is safe and secure.

Moreover, it's crucial to be careful about downloading apps and software onto your devices, as these can potentially be carriers of malware. **Only download apps from trusted sources**, such as the official app stores for your operating system, and make sure to read the reviews and ratings before downloading an app.

Lastly, it's important to **keep your device software up to date**, as these updates often include security fixes for known vulnerabilities. Keeping your device and software up-to-date will help ensure that your sensitive data remains protected.

As a conclusion, safeguarding sensitive data stored on personal devices requires a combination of common-sense precautions, such as using strong passwords and encryption, as well as being vigilant about downloading apps and software and keeping your devices and software up-to-date. By following these best practices, you can help protect your sensitive data and keep it safe from prying eyes.

Chapter 4. Protecting Business Data

Part 1: Securing Business Information: Importance and Risks

As businesses rely more and more on technology and data, protecting their information has become increasingly vital. A data breach can result in a loss of confidential information, harm to a company's reputation, and financial consequences. That is why it is imperative for businesses to understand the importance of protecting their data and the consequences of a data breach.

"The cost of a data breach has never been higher" says the 2020 Cost of a Data Breach Report by IBM Security. The average cost of a data breach for a company is now $3.86 million, with the financial industry being hit the hardest.

Here are four examples of high-profile data breaches that illustrate the importance of protecting business data:

Capital One (2019): In July 2019, a hacker accessed the personal information of over 100 million Capital One customers. The information included names, addresses, credit scores, and Social Security numbers. The cost of the data breach is estimated to be around $150 million.

Marriott International (2018): In November 2018, Marriott International announced that the personal information of 500 million guests had been stolen in a data breach. The information included names, addresses, phone numbers, email addresses, passport numbers, and payment card information. The cost of the breach was estimated to be around $124 million.

Equifax (2017): In September 2017, Equifax, one of the largest credit reporting agencies in the US, announced that the personal information of 143 million customers had been stolen in a data breach. The information included names, addresses, Social Security numbers, birth dates, and drivers' license numbers. The cost of the data breach was estimated to be around $439 million.

Target (2013): In December 2013, Target announced that the personal information of 40 million customers had been stolen in a data breach. The information included names, addresses, phone numbers, and payment card information. The cost of the data breach was estimated to be around $162 million.

These examples demonstrate the high cost and negative consequences that can result from a data breach. It is crucial for businesses to understand the importance of protecting their data and take the necessary steps to prevent breaches. This includes implementing strong security measures, regularly updating software and systems, and providing training for employees on data security best practices.

Part 2: Securing Business Networks

The significance of protecting business data continues to rise as the digital realm expands.

The consequences of a data breach can be catastrophic, ranging from financial losses to a tarnished reputation. It is essential that businesses implement the best practices for securing their networks to minimize the risk of a breach. In this section, we will discuss the best practices for securing business networks, including implementing firewalls, using encryption, and conducting regular security audits.

Implementing Firewalls

A firewall is a network security system that monitors and controls incoming and outgoing network traffic based on predetermined security rules. Firewalls are essential in protecting business networks from unauthorized access, hacking attempts, and other security threats. By implementing firewalls, businesses can protect their sensitive information, prevent data breaches, and maintain the integrity of their networks.

Using Encryption

Encryption is the process of converting plain text into a code that is only decipherable by authorized parties. By using encryption, businesses can protect their sensitive data and ensure that it is not accessible to unauthorized parties. Encryption can be applied to various forms of data, including emails, files, and databases. When using encryption, it is important to use strong encryption algorithms and keep the encryption keys secure.

Conducting Regular Security Audits

Regular security audits are critical for maintaining the security of a business network. During a security audit, a team of security experts examines the network for vulnerabilities, assesses the security measures in place, and provides recommendations for improvement. Regular security audits help businesses stay ahead of the latest security threats and ensure that their networks are protected.

By implementing firewalls, using encryption, and conducting regular security audits, businesses can protect their sensitive data and minimize the risk of a data breach. By staying ahead of the latest security threats, businesses can ensure the protection of their networks and maintain the trust of their customers.

Part 3: The Role of Employees in Protecting Business Data

In light of the rapid advancements in technology and the growing complexity of cyber threats, it becomes imperative for organizations to ensure that their personnel are adequately prepared to mitigate the risk of unauthorized access to confidential information. The need for employees to be equipped with the skills and knowledge necessary to safeguard sensitive data has become a critical aspect of contemporary business operations.

The role of employees in protecting business data cannot be overstated. A single mistake, such as clicking on a malicious link or using weak passwords, can result in a data breach that can cause significant financial and reputational harm to a company. This is why providing cybersecurity training to employees is crucial for the protection of business data.

One of the most effective ways to protect business data is to educate employees on the importance of cybersecurity and best practices for keeping information secure. In a report from the New York Times, it was noted that companies who invest in cybersecurity training for their employees often experience fewer data breaches and more secure networks. This is because employees are equipped with the knowledge and skills to recognize and respond to potential threats.

Awareness and education are crucial in the fight against cyberattacks. It's not just a matter of having the right technology in place, but also making sure that employees are trained to identify and prevent malicious activities.

Another benefit of providing cybersecurity training is that it helps to establish a culture of security within a company. This includes encouraging employees to report suspected incidents and promoting a shared responsibility for keeping data secure.

Examples of Effective Cybersecurity Training Programs

Simulated Phishing Attacks: One effective way to train employees is to conduct simulated phishing attacks. This involves sending fake phishing emails to employees and monitoring their responses. Those who fall for the fake emails receive additional training to help them recognize and avoid similar attacks in the future.

Role-Playing Scenarios: Another effective method of training is to use role-playing scenarios that simulate real-world cyber threats. This allows employees to practice their response to a potential breach and helps them to better understand the impact of their actions on the security of sensitive data.

Interactive Online Training: Interactive online training programs are another effective method for providing cybersecurity training. These programs often use gamification techniques to make learning about cybersecurity more engaging and enjoyable for employees.

Regular Refresher Courses: Regular refresher courses are also important for maintaining the effectiveness of cybersecurity training. As new threats emerge, it's crucial to ensure that employees are updated on the latest best practices and strategies for keeping data secure.

To sum up, the role of employees in protecting business data is crucial. Providing cybersecurity training to employees is one of the most effective ways to ensure the security of sensitive data. From simulated phishing attacks to role-playing scenarios and interactive online training, there are many effective methods for providing this type of education. By establishing a culture of security within a company and regularly updating employees on the latest best practices, businesses can help to minimize the risk of a data breach and protect their sensitive information.

Chapter 5. Preventing Cyberattacks

Part 1: Steps to Prevent Cyberattacks

In the current technologically advanced landscape, cyber attacks are a prevalent phenomenon that pose a significant risk to both individuals and organizations. The annual frequency of these attacks has seen a consistent upward trend, highlighting the importance of taking proactive measures to protect against them. It is imperative to take steps to prevent these attacks and protect your sensitive information. The following are some of the best practices for preventing cyberattacks:

Use strong passwords: One of the most basic steps to prevent cyberattacks is to use strong passwords. A strong password should be at least 12 characters long and include a mix of letters, numbers, and special characters. Avoid using easily guessable information, such as your name or birthdate, as part of your password.

Keep software up-to-date: Software developers constantly release updates to fix vulnerabilities in their products. It is important to keep all software, including operating systems and applications, up-to-date to prevent attackers from exploiting these vulnerabilities.

Avoid suspicious emails and websites: Phishing scams are a common way for cybercriminals to trick people into giving away sensitive information. Be cautious when opening emails or visiting websites, especially if they look suspicious or contain unexpected attachments. If you receive an email that asks for your password or other sensitive information, be sure to verify the sender's identity before responding.

Use anti-virus software: Anti-virus software is designed to detect and prevent malware from infecting your device. It is important to have up-to-date anti-virus software installed on all devices to protect against cyberattacks.

To bring it all together, it can be stated that in order to effectively mitigate the risks associated with cyberattacks, it is imperative to maintain a persistent focus on vigilance and attention to detail. By following the best practices outlined above, you can significantly reduce your risk of falling victim to a cyberattack. Keep in mind that security is a process, not a product. By staying informed and taking proactive steps to protect your information, you can help keep your data safe from cyberattacks.

Part 2: The Importance of Cybersecurity Training

In addition to the steps outlined above, providing cybersecurity training for employees is crucial in preventing cyberattacks. Employees are often the first line of defense against cyberattacks, and it is essential that they are aware of the threats and know how to identify and respond to them. Here are a few key reasons why cybersecurity training is important:

Awareness: Cybersecurity training helps employees understand the importance of protecting sensitive information and how they can play a role in preventing cyberattacks. They learn about the types of cyberattacks, how they can occur, and how to recognize warning signs.

Responsibility: Employees who are trained in cybersecurity take their responsibilities seriously and understand the critical role they play in protecting the company's data and systems. This increased sense of responsibility can lead to better security practices and a stronger overall security posture.

Risk reduction: By providing cybersecurity training, companies can reduce the risk of cyberattacks by educating employees on how to recognize and avoid potential threats. This reduces the likelihood of employees falling for phishing scams or other types of cyberattacks, which can have significant consequences for the company.

Cybersecurity training is essential for employees to understand the role they play in protecting the company's data and systems. It is an investment that can pay off by reducing the risk of cyberattacks and helping employees to identify and respond to potential threats. Providing regular cybersecurity training can help to ensure that employees are aware of the latest threats and can make informed decisions about protecting the company's sensitive information.

One of the most significant security risks is social engineering, and the most effective method of defense against it is through education and heightened awareness. By investing in cybersecurity training for employees, companies can better protect their sensitive information and reduce the risk of cyberattacks.

Part 3: The Role of Cybersecurity Professionals in Preventing Cyberattacks

Cybersecurity is a rapidly evolving field, and it can be difficult for individuals or organizations to stay up-to-date with the latest threats and best practices. This is where cybersecurity professionals come in. These experts are trained to identify and mitigate cyber risks, and they play a critical role in preventing cyberattacks.

Hiring a cybersecurity professional to assess your security risks is an important step in protecting your organization from cyberattacks. A professional will be able to identify any vulnerabilities in your systems and help you develop a comprehensive security plan to address these issues. They can also provide ongoing support and guidance to ensure that your systems remain secure.

Regular security audits and penetration testing are also important components of a comprehensive cybersecurity strategy. During a security audit, a professional will review your systems and processes to identify any potential security threats. Penetration testing involves simulating a real-world cyberattack to identify vulnerabilities in your systems. These assessments can be conducted by internal staff or by hiring a professional to provide an independent evaluation.

To put it succinctly, the role of cybersecurity professionals in preventing cyberattacks is critical. By hiring a professional to assess your security risks and conducting regular security audits and penetration testing, you can be confident that your systems are secure and your sensitive information is protected. By working with a cybersecurity professional and implementing best practices, you can help ensure the security of your organization's data.

Chapter 6. Detecting Cyberattacks

Part 1: Detecting the Signs of a Cyberattack

Cyberattacks can have a significant impact on an organization, which is why it is important to detect them as quickly as possible. The following are some of the signs that a cyberattack may be underway:

Unusual activity on a network: Cyberattacks often result in unusual network activity, such as a sudden increase in network traffic, the appearance of new devices on the network, or unusual patterns of data transfer. Cybersecurity professionals monitor network activity to detect any anomalies that may indicate a cyberattack is underway.

Slow performance: Cyberattacks can also slow down a network or individual devices, causing slow performance or even crashes. If you notice that your network or devices are suddenly running slower than usual, it may be a sign of a cyberattack.

Unusual emails: Phishing scams are a common form of cyberattack, and often come in the form of suspicious emails. Be on the lookout for emails that contain unexpected attachments or requests for sensitive information, as these may be signs of a phishing attack.

Cyberattacks can strike at any time, which is why it is important to remain vigilant and be able to recognize the signs of an attack. Early detection of a cyberattack is crucial in minimizing the damage it can cause.

To conclude, recognizing the signs of a cyberattack is an important step in detecting and responding to threats. By staying informed and being aware of the signs of a cyberattack, you can help protect your organization from the damage it can cause. Early detection is vital to defending against cyberattacks. A delay in response, even just for a minute, can result in significant damage to a company's revenue, reputation, and confidential information.

PART 2: TOOLS AND TECHNIQUES FOR DETECTING CYBERATTACKS

The role of cybersecurity professionals in detecting cyberattacks is vital, and to aid in their efforts, a variety of tools and technologies have been developed. These tools allow for real-time monitoring of networks, the identification of suspicious activity, and the rapid response to threats.

One commonly used tool is an intrusion detection system (IDS), which is designed to detect unauthorized access to a network. It's an essential component of a comprehensive security strategy as they provide real-time monitoring and analysis of network activity.

Another key tool used by cybersecurity professionals is network monitoring software. This software is used to monitor network traffic and identify any unusual or suspicious activity. Continuous monitoring of networks is essential in identifying cyberattacks, as it provides security experts with the ability to instantly observe network activities.

In addition to IDS and network monitoring software, cybersecurity professionals also utilize security information and event management (SIEM) systems. SIEM systems allow for the centralization and correlation of security-related data from multiple sources, making it easier for security professionals to detect and respond to threats.

Finally, honeypots and honeynets are also used by cybersecurity professionals as a means of detecting cyberattacks. A honeypot is a decoy system that is set up to attract and detect malicious activity, while a honeynet is a network of honeypots.

In closing, cybersecurity professionals rely on a variety of tools to detect and respond to cyberattacks, including intrusion detection systems, network monitoring software, SIEM systems, and honeypots and honeynets. These tools play a crucial role in protecting networks and systems from cyber threats.

Part 3: Preparing for a Cyberattack: Developing an Effective Response Plan

Cyberattacks can be devastating for organizations, causing financial loss, damage to reputation, and loss of sensitive information. For this reason, it is crucial to have a well-designed plan in place to respond to cyberattacks effectively and minimize the damage they can cause. Cybersecurity is not a problem that can be solved by any one company, any one government, or any one organization. This highlights the need for collaboration and cooperation between various stakeholders, including cybersecurity professionals, to develop a comprehensive response plan.

A well-designed response plan should include the following elements:

Identification of the types of cyberattacks the organization is likely to face

Designation of specific roles and responsibilities for responding to a cyberattack

Development of procedures for containing and mitigating the impact of a cyberattack

Establishment of protocols for communicating with stakeholders, including employees, customers, and the media, during and after a cyberattack.

Cybersecurity professionals play a critical role in detecting and responding to cyberattacks. They use a range of tools and techniques, including intrusion detection systems and network monitoring software, to monitor networks and systems for signs of an attack.

The traditional concept of a secure perimeter has evolved. In the past, the network was considered safe and the potential threats were believed to lie outside of it. Nowadays, the network itself presents a potential hazard. This highlights the need for cybersecurity professionals to be proactive in detecting and responding to threats and to be aware of the changing nature of cyberattacks.

In essence, having a well-designed plan in place for responding to a cyberattack is essential for organizations to minimize the damage that these attacks can cause. Cybersecurity professionals play a critical role in detecting and responding to threats, and their expertise and knowledge are invaluable in developing and implementing an effective response plan.

Chapter 7. Responding Effectively to Cyberattacks

Part 1: Immediate Response Measures for Mitigating the Effects of a Cyberattack

It is imperative to be prepared to respond effectively to minimize the damage caused by these attacks. When a cyberattack occurs, the first step is to isolate the affected systems and conduct a forensic investigation to determine the cause and extent of the breach. This helps to prevent the attacker from spreading to other systems and causing further damage.

One of the key principles of responding to a cyberattack is to **"contain, eradicate, and recover"** as stated by Michael Assante, the former CSO at the North American Electric Reliability Corporation. This involves isolating the affected systems, eliminating the source of the attack, and restoring normal operations as quickly and efficiently as possible.

In order to achieve this, organizations must have a well-defined incident **response plan** in place. This plan should outline the steps that need to be taken in the event of a cyberattack, including who is responsible for different tasks, how to communicate with stakeholders, and how to coordinate with law enforcement and other agencies.

One important aspect of the incident response plan is to **isolate the affected systems**. This involves disconnecting the systems from the network to prevent the attacker from accessing or damaging them further. This also helps to preserve any evidence that may be needed for the forensic investigation.

The forensic investigation is an important part of the response process as it provides valuable insights into the cause and extent of the breach. Cybersecurity professionals use a variety of tools and techniques to collect and analyze data from the affected systems, including network logs, system images, and memory dumps. This information is then used to determine the cause of the breach and identify any vulnerabilities that may have been exploited by the attacker.

Once the investigation is complete, the next step is to **restore normal operations**. This may involve patching any vulnerabilities that were exploited, updating software and security systems, and monitoring the network for any unusual activity.

To wrap up, the initial response to a cyberattack is a critical part of the overall security strategy, and organizations must be prepared to respond effectively to minimize the damage caused by these attacks. With a well-defined incident response plan, organizations can ensure that the right steps are taken at the right time to contain the attack, eliminate the source, and restore normal operations as quickly as possible.

Part 2: Reporting Cyberattacks and the Role of Cybersecurity Professionals

While there are many steps that can be taken to prevent and respond to cyberattacks, reporting these incidents to law enforcement is an important part of the process. Reporting cyberattacks can help organizations and individuals to understand the nature and extent of the threat, as well as provide valuable information to law enforcement that can be used to investigate and resolve the incident.

In order to effectively report cyberattacks, it is important to have a clear understanding of the role of cybersecurity professionals in responding to these incidents. These professionals are typically responsible for identifying and responding to security incidents, as well as conducting investigations into the causes of these incidents and developing strategies for preventing similar attacks in the future.

For example, a cybersecurity professional might be tasked with analyzing the affected systems and networks, collecting and analyzing data related to the incident, and communicating with law enforcement and other stakeholders. They may also work closely with other members of the organization, including IT teams and legal experts, to develop and implement a response plan that is tailored to the specific needs and requirements of the organization.

Cybersecurity is not a problem that can be solved by any one company, any one government, or any one organization. It requires a collective effort to defend against cyber threats. This highlights the importance of working with cybersecurity professionals who have the expertise and knowledge needed to respond effectively to cyberattacks and resolve security incidents.

Therefore, it is crucial for organizations and individuals to understand the importance of reporting cyberattacks to law enforcement and the role of cybersecurity professionals in responding to and resolving these incidents. With their skills and experience, cybersecurity professionals play a vital role in helping organizations and individuals to protect their sensitive information and assets from cyber threats.

Part 3: Comprehensive Measures for Preventing Future Cyberattacks

Preventing future cyberattacks requires a multi-layered approach that combines technology, policies, and employee training. This is according to a book on cybersecurity, which highlights the importance of taking proactive measures to secure sensitive information and systems.

Implementing comprehensive security measures is crucial in deterring unauthorized access to sensitive information. This includes the deployment of firewalls, antivirus software, intrusion detection systems, and other security tools that are designed to detect and prevent cyberattacks.

Regular security audits play a vital role in ensuring the continued protection of an organization's systems. These audits can help identify potential vulnerabilities and provide a comprehensive assessment of the organization's current security posture. Audits can include testing the strength of passwords, reviewing the organization's network architecture, and verifying the integrity of data backups.

Organizations must stay vigilant and proactively work to secure their systems to stay ahead of constantly evolving cyber threats. Implementing strong security measures and regularly reviewing and updating these measures can greatly reduce the risk of a successful cyberattack. Employee training also plays a crucial role in preventing cyberattacks, as employees are often the first line of defense against cyber threats. By providing employees with the knowledge and skills to identify and respond to potential cyber threats, organizations can significantly reduce the risk of a successful attack.

To summarize, preventing future cyberattacks requires a comprehensive and proactive approach that combines technology, policies, and employee training. Regular security audits and the implementation of strong security measures are key components of an effective cybersecurity strategy. Organizations must stay vigilant and continuously work to secure their systems to stay ahead of evolving cyber threats.

Chapter 8. Cybersecurity Trends and Developments

Part 1: Exploring the Emerging Trends and Advancements in Cybersecurity

In recent years, the field of cybersecurity has rapidly evolved and advanced. The increasing reliance on technology, the proliferation of connected devices, and the growing sophistication of cyber threats have all contributed to the growing importance of cybersecurity. As such, it is crucial for organizations to stay abreast of the latest trends and developments in the field. In this section, we will explore some of the most significant trends and developments in cybersecurity, including cloud security, artificial intelligence, and the Internet of Things (IoT).

Cloud Security

One of the biggest trends in cybersecurity is the increasing use of cloud computing. Cloud computing allows organizations to store and access their data and applications over the internet, rather than on local servers or devices. This provides many benefits, including increased efficiency, scalability, and cost savings. However, it also introduces new security challenges, as sensitive data is stored on third-party servers that are often beyond the control of the organization.

To address these security concerns, cloud service providers have implemented various security measures, including encryption, access controls, and auditing. In addition, many organizations are adopting best practices for cloud security, such as performing regular security assessments, implementing multi-factor authentication, and using encryption to protect sensitive data.

Artificial Intelligence

Another important trend in cybersecurity is the increasing use of artificial intelligence (AI). AI is being used in a variety of ways to enhance security, including intrusion detection and prevention, network security, and threat intelligence. For example, AI can be used to identify and respond to threats in real-time, to analyze large amounts of security data to identify patterns and anomalies, and to automate repetitive tasks, freeing up security personnel to focus on more strategic tasks.

However, AI also introduces new risks, as it can be used by attackers to carry out sophisticated attacks. For example, AI can be used to automate the process of compromising systems, to evade security measures, and to create convincing phishing emails. To mitigate these risks, organizations must carefully manage the deployment of AI in their security programs, ensuring that it is properly trained, monitored, and controlled.

Internet of Things (IoT)

The Internet of Things (IoT) is another important trend in cybersecurity, as the proliferation of connected devices continues to grow. IoT devices, such as smart home devices, wearables, and industrial control systems, can provide tremendous benefits, but they also introduce new security risks. For example, many IoT devices have limited processing power, memory, and storage, making it difficult to secure them properly. In addition, many IoT devices use proprietary protocols and are often beyond the control of the organization.

To address these security concerns, organizations must implement strong security measures for IoT devices, such as encryption, access controls, and software updates. In addition, organizations must be vigilant about the security of IoT devices, regularly monitoring and assessing their security posture and implementing best practices for securing these devices.

In final analysis, the field of cybersecurity is rapidly evolving, and organizations must stay abreast of the latest trends and developments in order to effectively secure their systems and data. By understanding and effectively addressing the security challenges posed by cloud computing, artificial intelligence, and the Internet of Things, organizations can build strong, resilient security programs that can effectively protect against cyber threats.

Part 2: Navigating the Evolving Landscape of Cybersecurity: Understanding the Impacts and Opportunities of Emerging Trends

In Part 1 of this chapter, we embarked on a comprehensive exploration of the cutting-edge trends and advancements in the field of cybersecurity, including cloud computing, artificial intelligence, and the Internet of Things (IoT). In Part 2, we will delve into the intricacies of the challenges and opportunities that these emerging trends present for businesses and individuals alike.

Businesses face a multitude of challenges when it comes to adopting and implementing new technologies, particularly in the realm of cybersecurity. The implementation of these technologies often requires a significant investment of financial resources and time to upgrade existing systems and processes. Furthermore, the rapid pace of technological change often means that businesses must continuously educate themselves to stay ahead of the latest advancements and developments in the field. Despite these challenges, businesses that are willing to invest the time and resources required to properly understand and implement these technologies can reap substantial benefits. For instance, the deployment of cloud computing can greatly enhance efficiency and scalability, while the use of artificial intelligence can automate many repetitive tasks, freeing up valuable resources and reducing the risk of human error.

Individuals also face their own unique challenges as they navigate the rapidly changing landscape of cybersecurity. They must remain vigilant and aware of the latest threats, such as phishing scams and other forms of malicious activity, and take the necessary steps to protect their personal information, such as using strong passwords and being wary of suspicious emails or websites. However, there are also numerous opportunities for individuals in the field of cybersecurity. Advances in technology have made it easier for individuals to access and use online security tools, and there has been a growing trend towards the development of more secure forms of digital payment.

The challenges and opportunities presented by emerging trends in cybersecurity are complex and varied. Both businesses and individuals must be proactive in their approach, staying informed and taking the necessary steps to safeguard their assets. By doing so, they can confidently navigate the rapidly evolving landscape of cybersecurity and reap the benefits of these cutting-edge technologies.

Part 3: Staying Ahead of the Game: The Importance of Staying Current in Cybersecurity Trends

As technology continues to advance and the digital landscape broadens, cybersecurity threats are becoming increasingly sophisticated and widespread. In order to stay protected against these threats, it is crucial for individuals, businesses, and cybersecurity professionals to stay up-to-date on the latest trends and developments in the field. In this section, we will discuss the importance of staying informed and the role of cybersecurity professionals in staying ahead of the curve.

One of the most significant challenges in cybersecurity is the pace of change. As new technologies are developed and new threats emerge, cybersecurity professionals must be able to adapt and respond quickly in order to protect their networks and assets. This requires a constant commitment to staying informed and knowledgeable about the latest developments in the field. For businesses, this can mean investing in the right tools and resources to keep their systems and data secure, as well as regularly training employees on cybersecurity best practices.

Cybersecurity professionals play a critical role in staying ahead of the curve by staying informed and knowledgeable about the latest threats and technologies. This requires ongoing education and training, as well as staying up-to-date on the latest trends and developments in the field. In addition, cybersecurity professionals must also be proactive in identifying and mitigating new threats, as well as working with organizations to develop and implement effective cybersecurity strategies.

One important way for cybersecurity professionals to stay ahead of the curve is by participating **in industry events and conferences**, such as the RSA Conference or the Black Hat conference. These events provide opportunities to network with other professionals, learn about new technologies and strategies, and stay informed about the latest threats and trends in the field.

In addition, cybersecurity professionals can also stay informed by **reading industry publications**, such as Dark Reading or Information Security, or by following thought leaders and experts in the field on social media. By staying informed and engaged with the latest trends and developments in the field, cybersecurity professionals can remain at the forefront of their industry and be better equipped to protect their organizations and assets.

However, staying informed and up-to-date is not just important for cybersecurity professionals. Businesses must also take an active role in staying informed and taking steps to protect their assets. This includes regularly conducting **risk assessments and vulnerability scans**, as well as implementing effective security solutions, such as firewalls, intrusion detection systems, and encryption technologies.

Individuals also play a crucial role in staying informed and protected. This can mean regularly **updating software** and applications, **using strong passwords** and **two-factor authentication**, and **being wary of phishing** scams and other cyberattacks. By staying informed and taking proactive steps to protect their assets, individuals can play an important role in ensuring the security and integrity of the digital world.

In final thoughts, staying up-to-date on the latest trends and developments in cybersecurity is essential for individuals, businesses, and cybersecurity professionals alike. Whether through ongoing education and training, participating in industry events, or taking steps to protect personal assets, staying informed and proactive is the key to staying ahead of the curve in the rapidly evolving landscape of cybersecurity. By staying ahead of the game, we can help ensure the security and integrity of the digital world and protect against the growing threat of cyberattacks.

www.ingramcontent.com/pod-product-compliance
Lightning Source LLC
Chambersburg PA
CBHW050300220526
45465CB00002B/754